DAWN & DUSK

IMPRESSIONS FROM ATWOOD

ECHO HILL ARTS PRESS

COPYRIGHT 2017
ISBN: 978-0-9995061-0-3

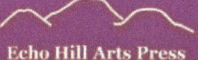

Echo Hill Arts Press

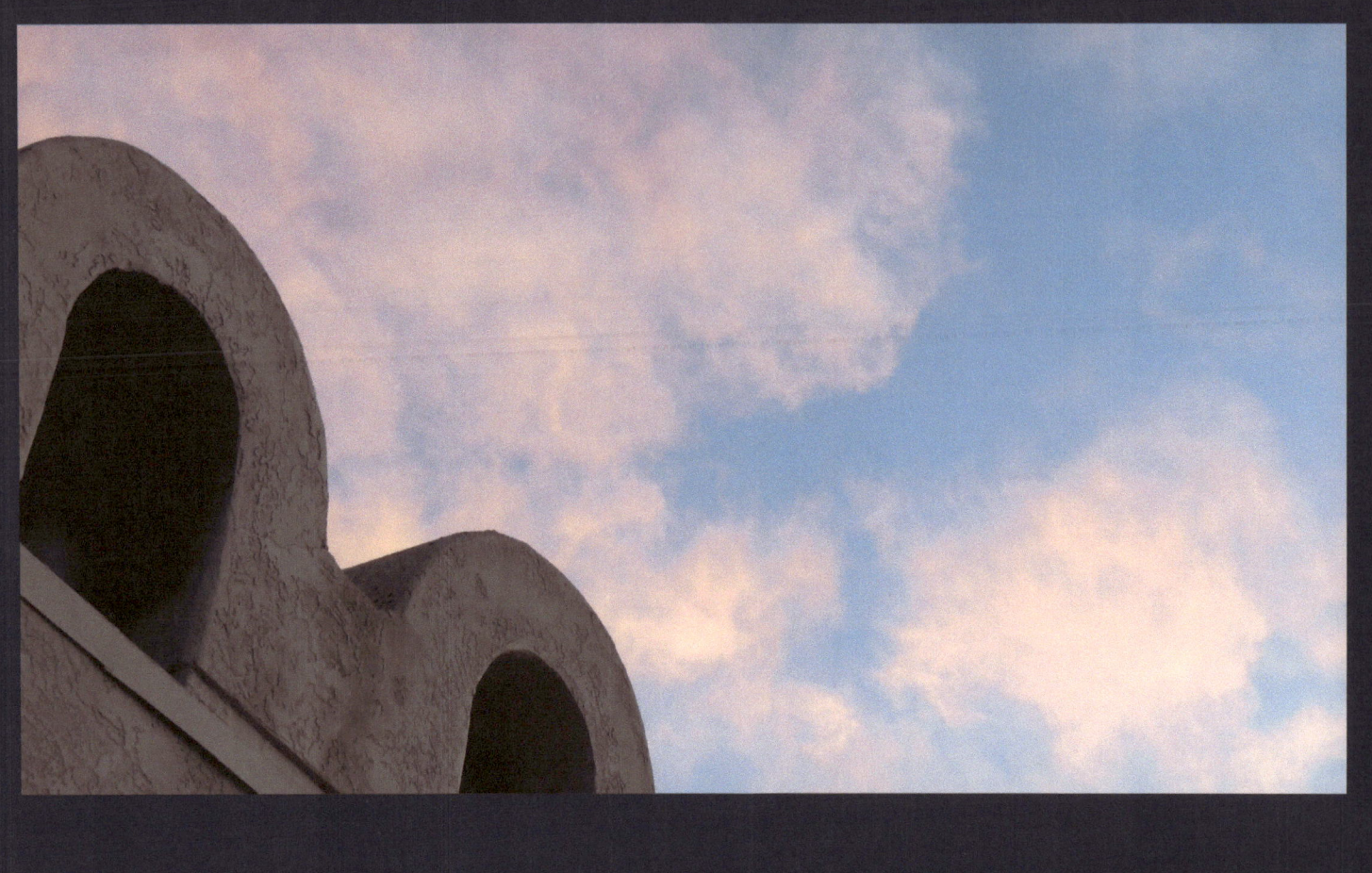

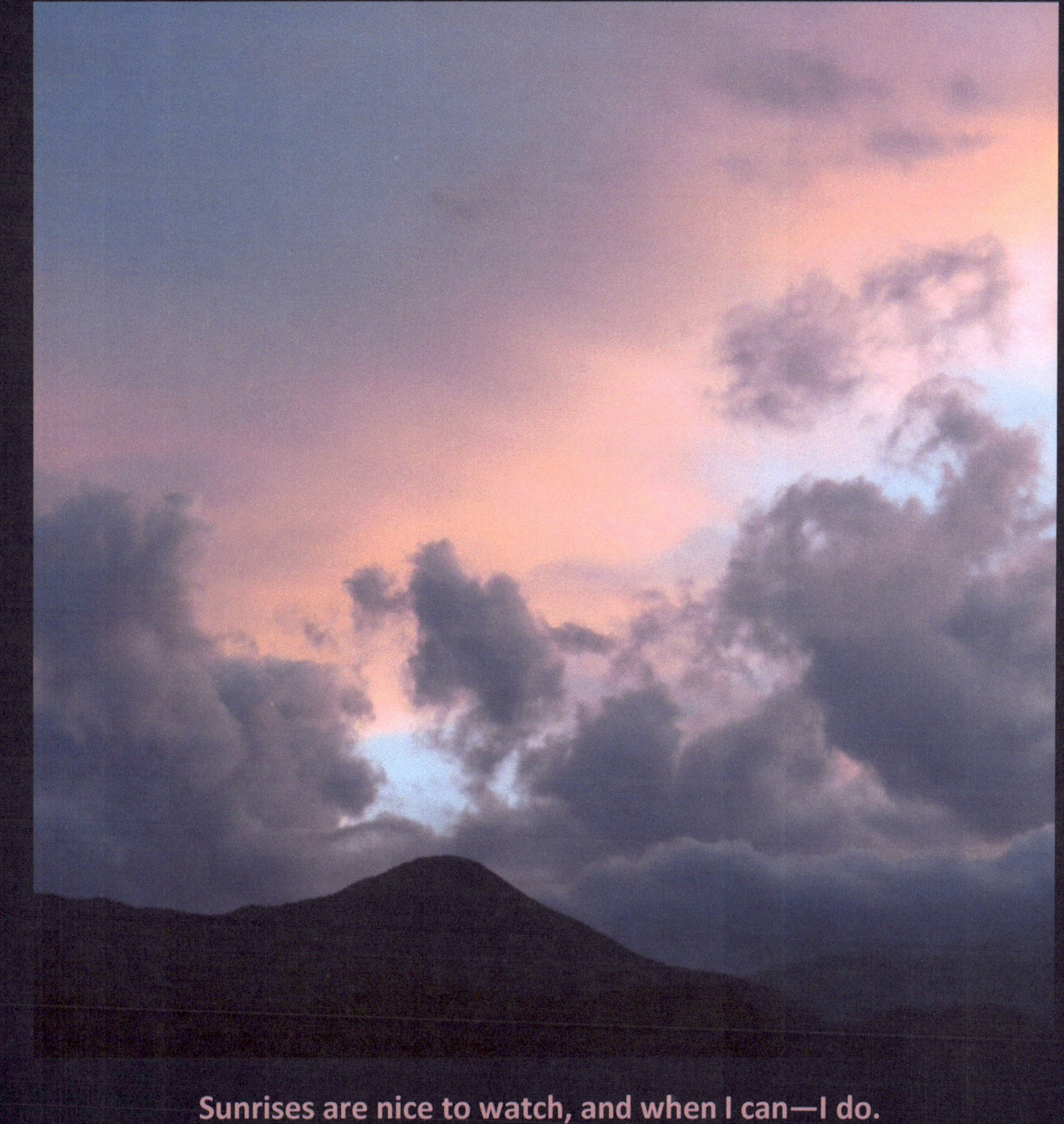

Sunrises are nice to watch, and when I can—I do.

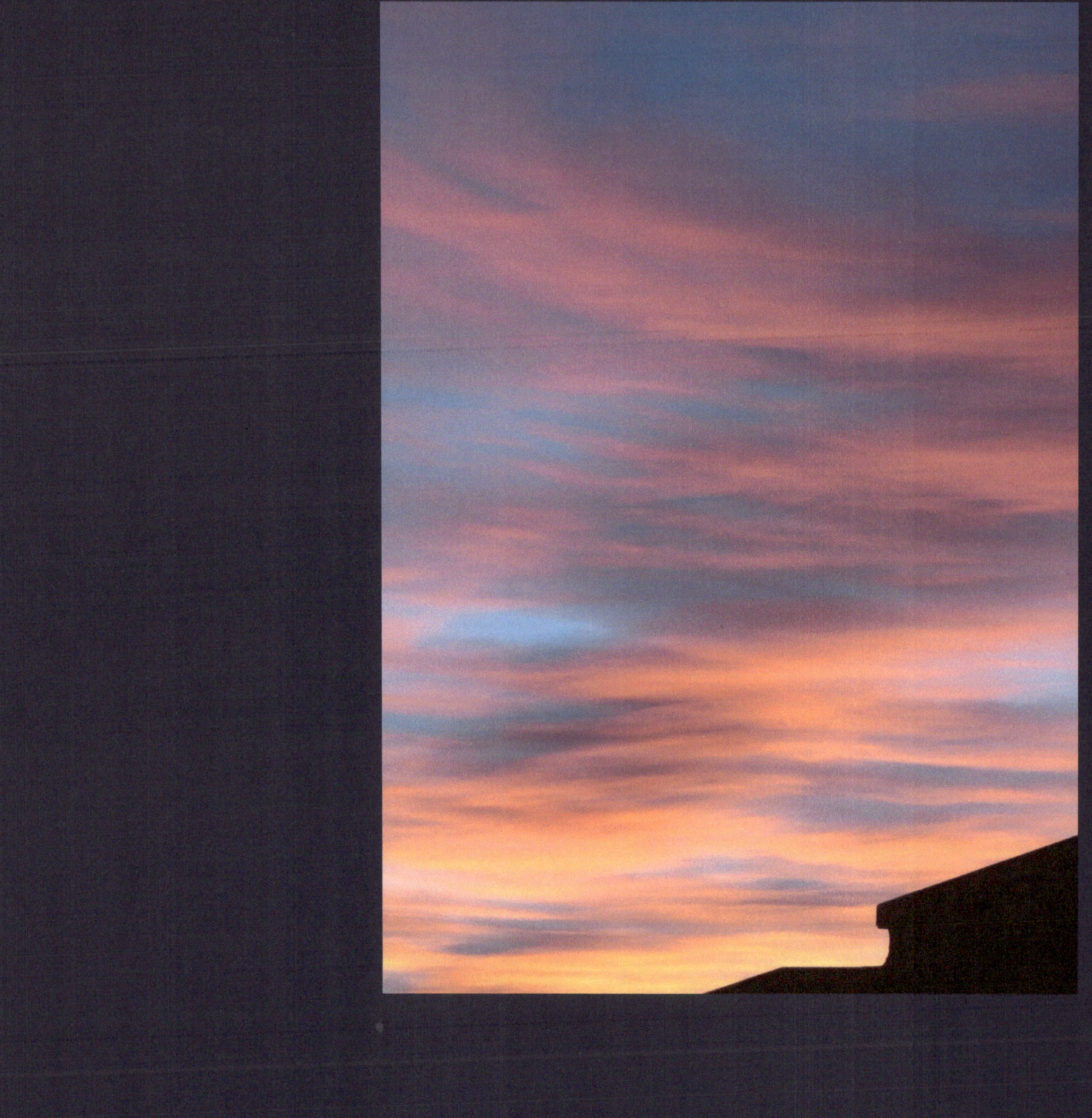

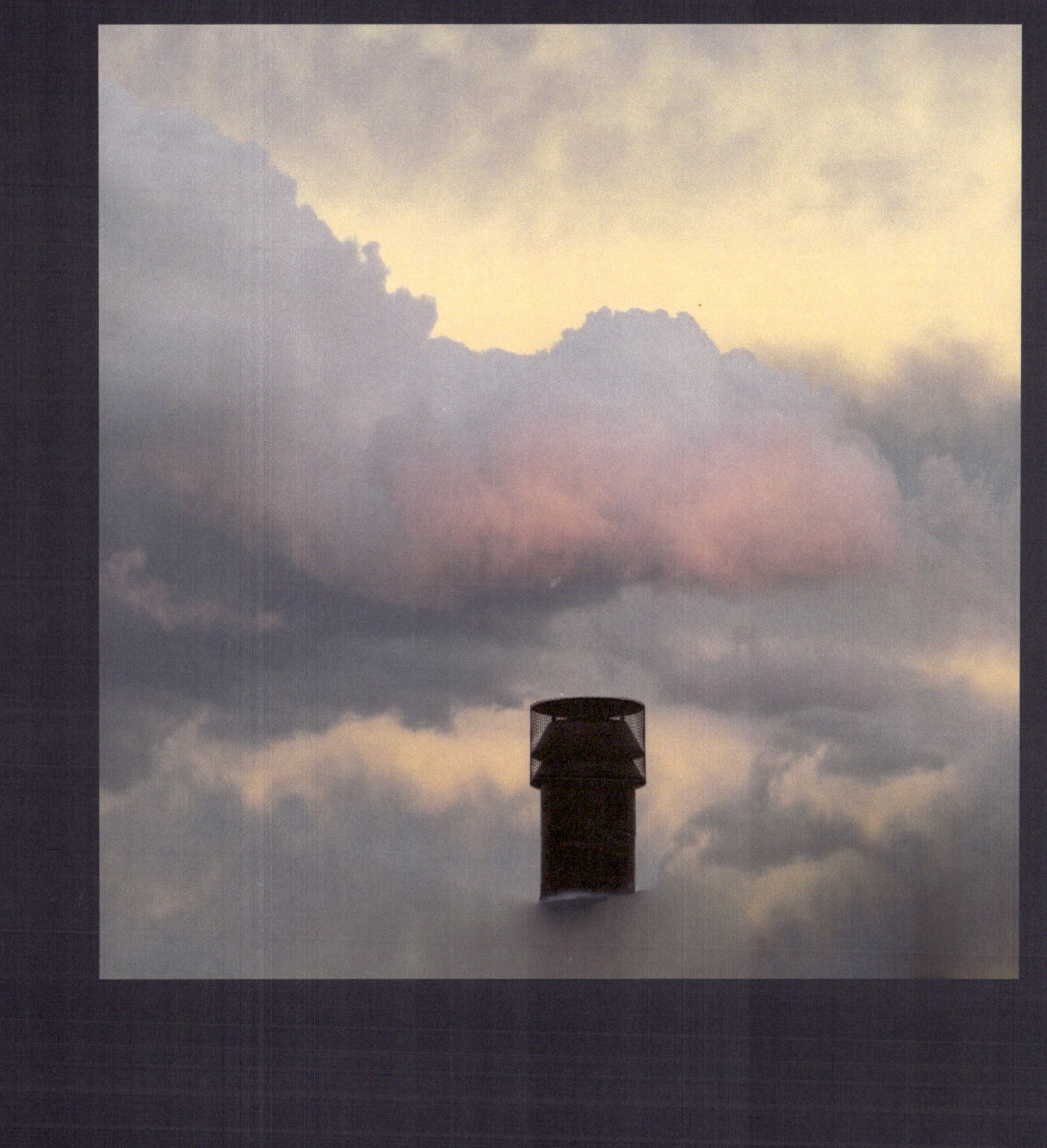

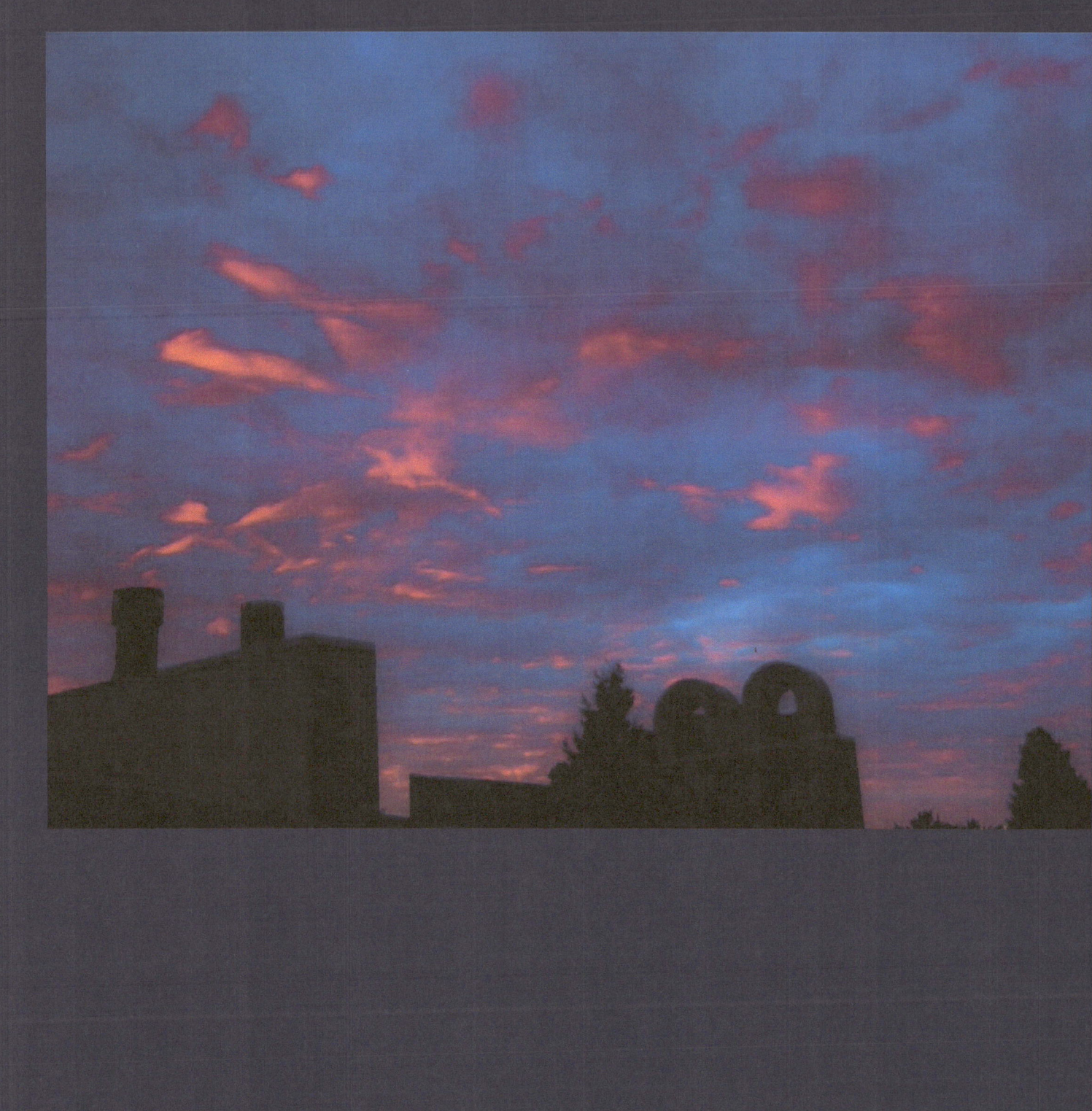

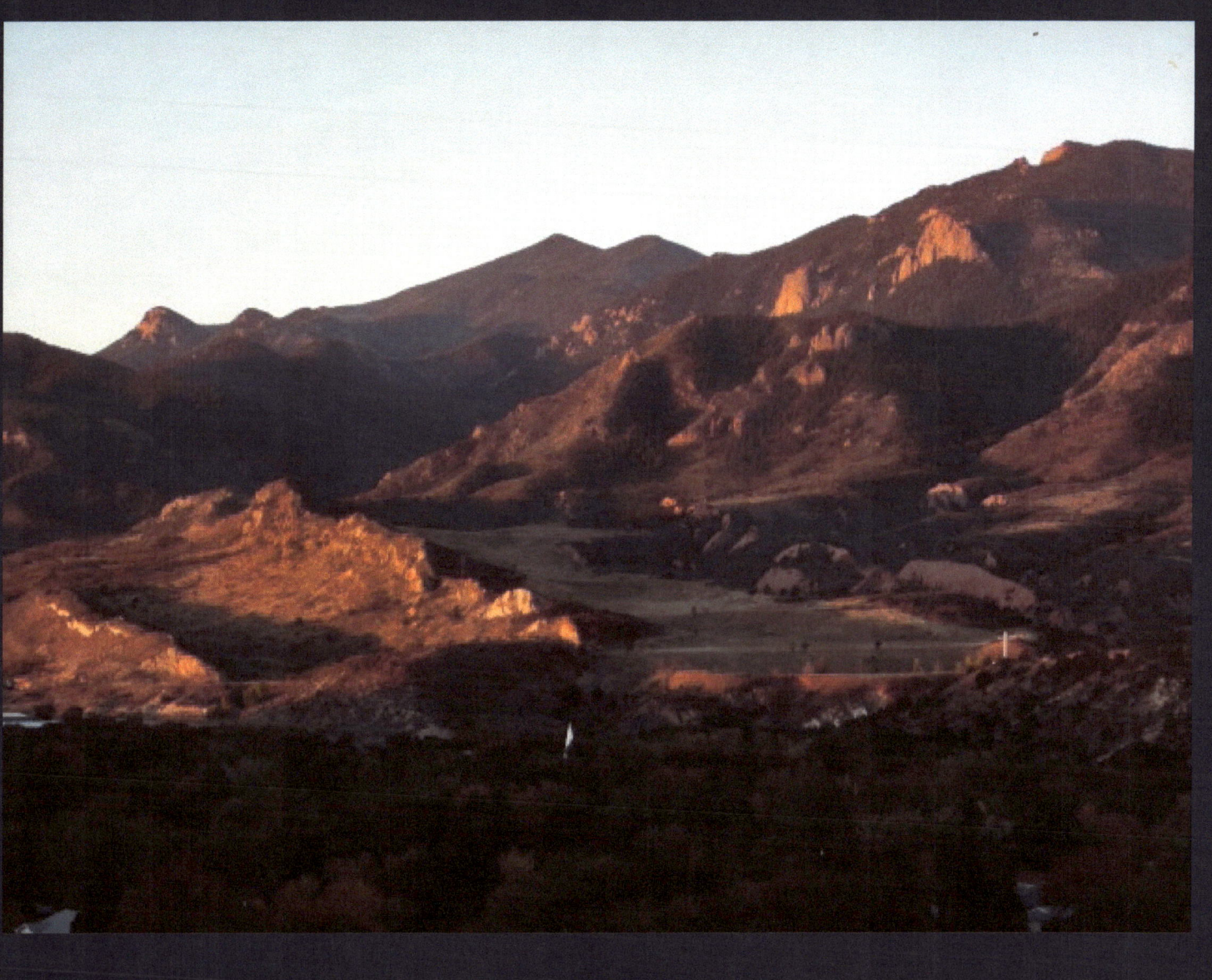

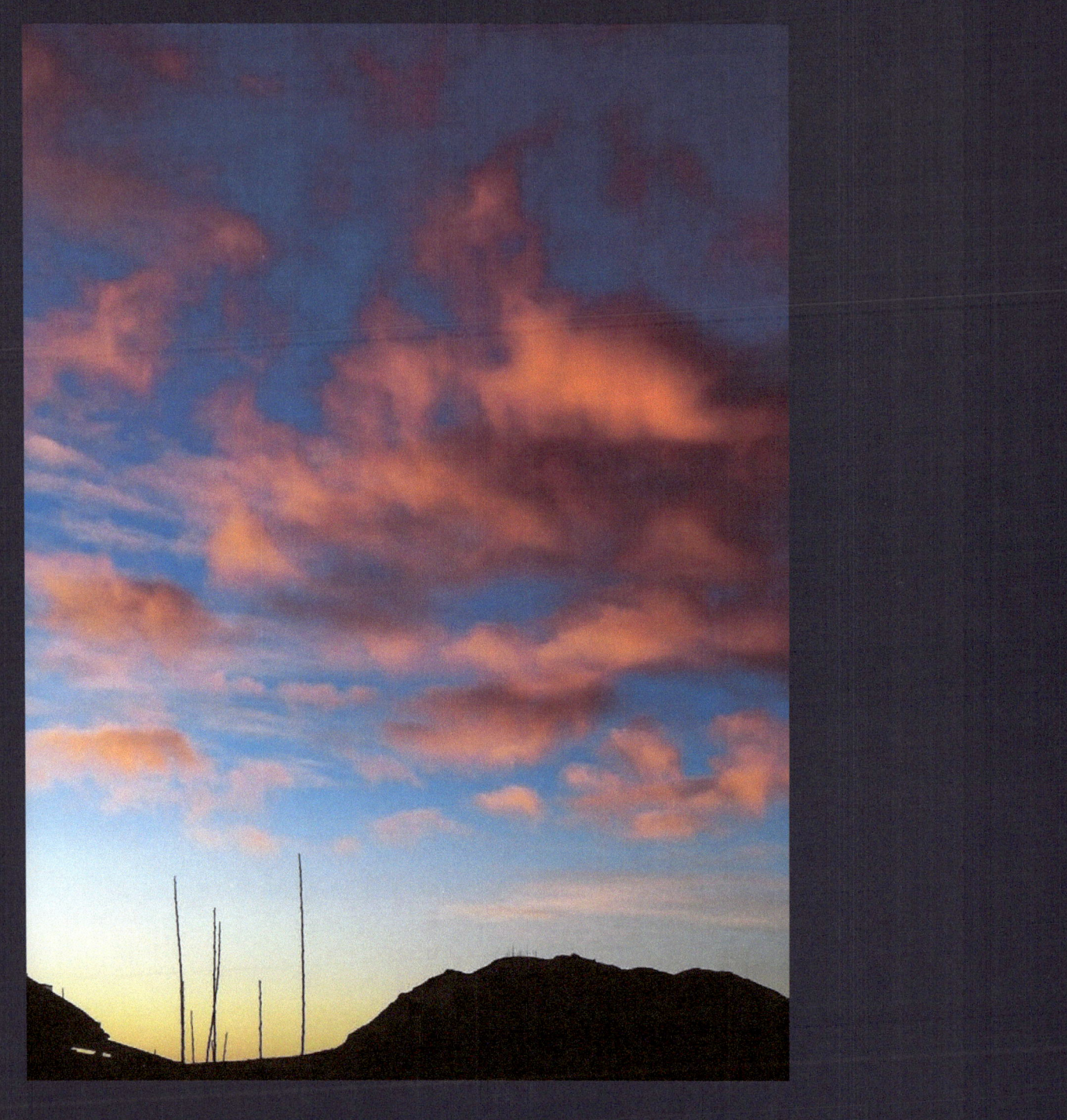

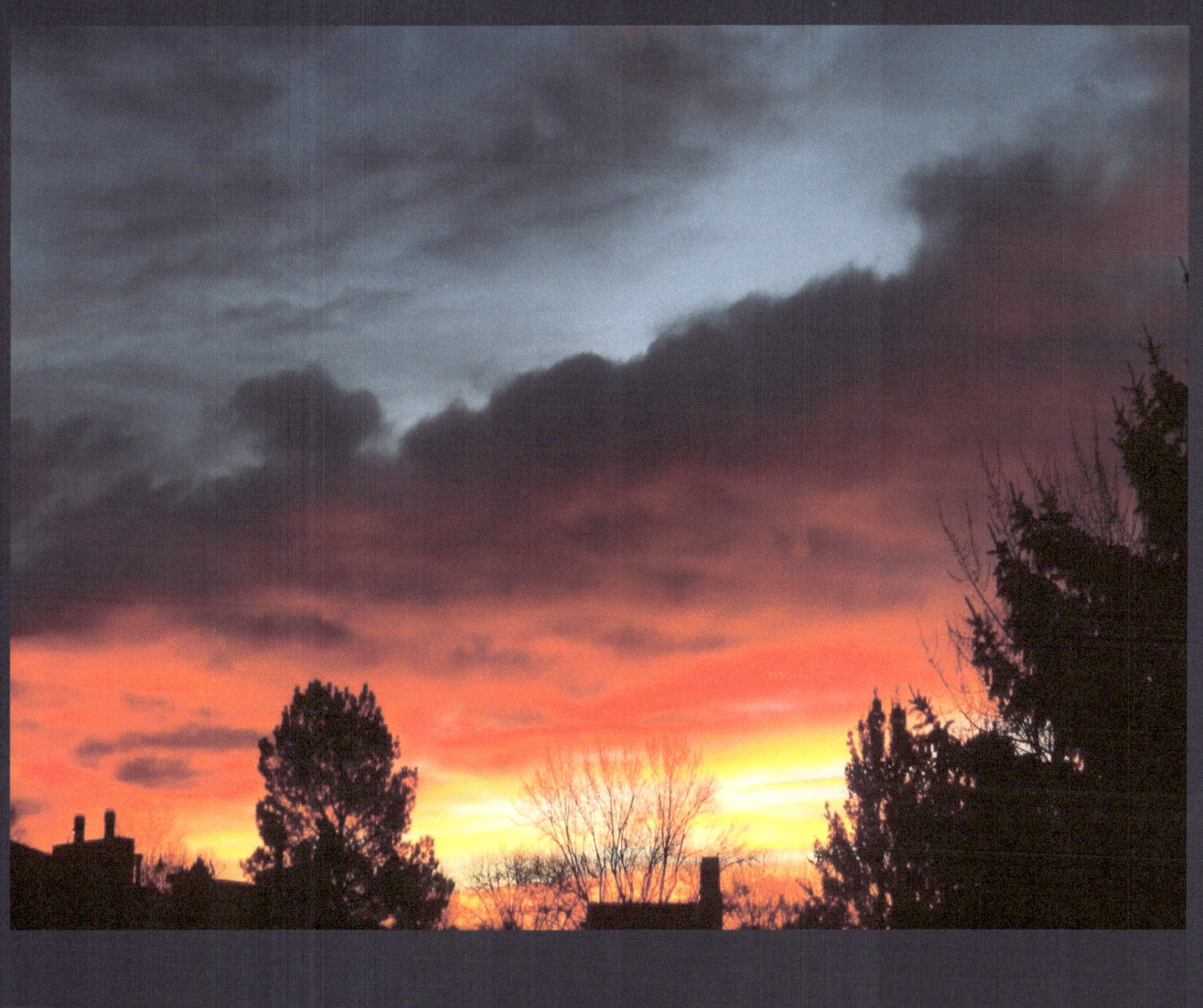

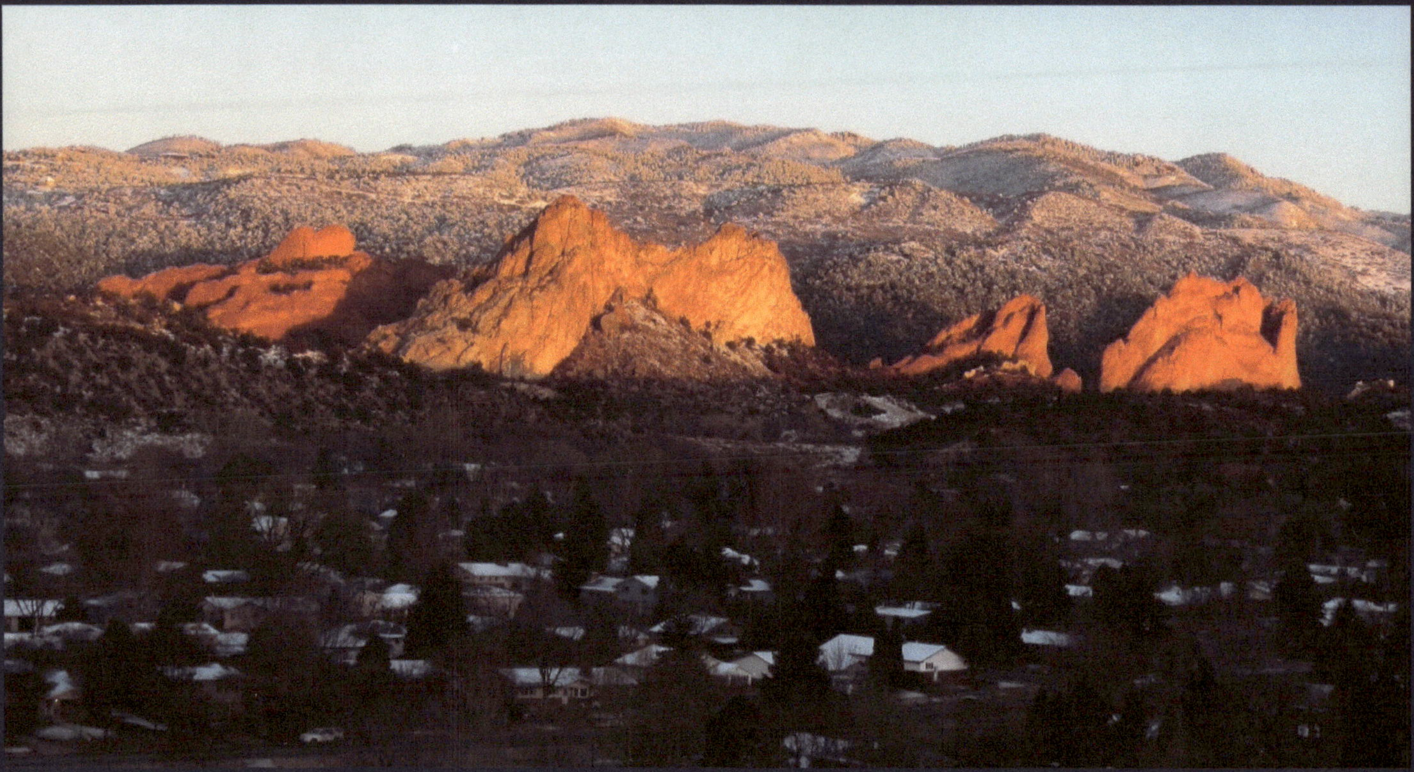

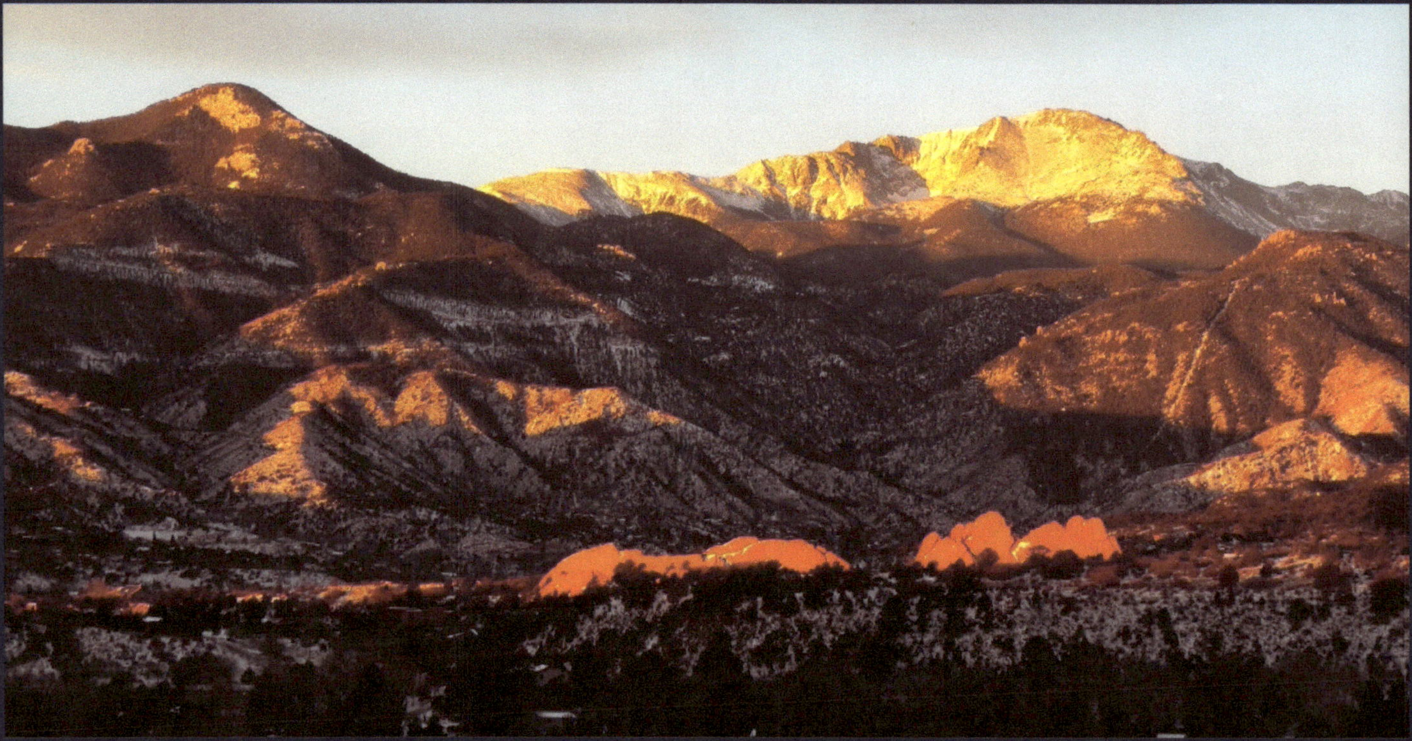

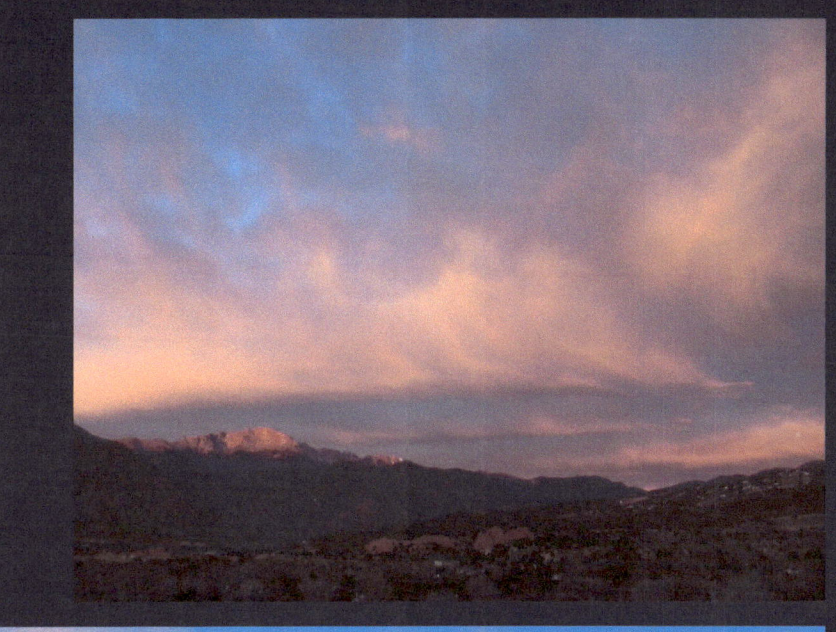

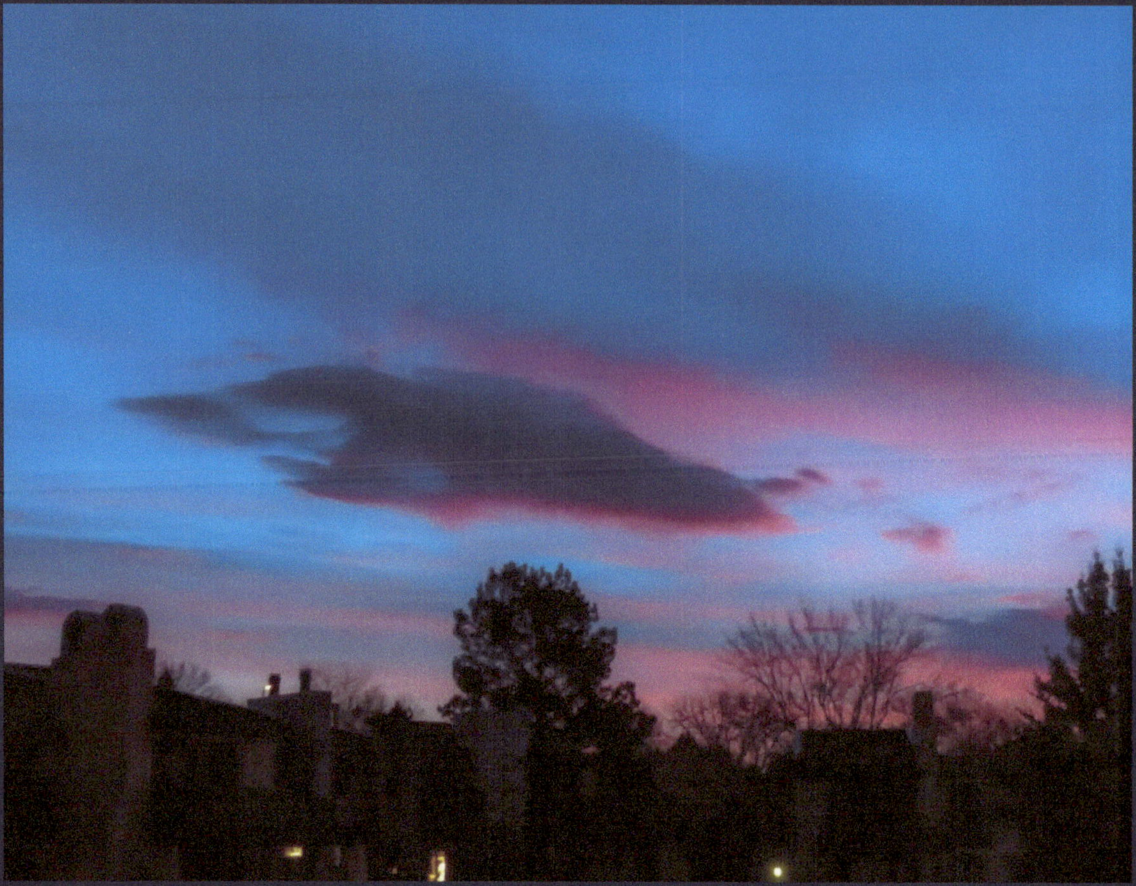

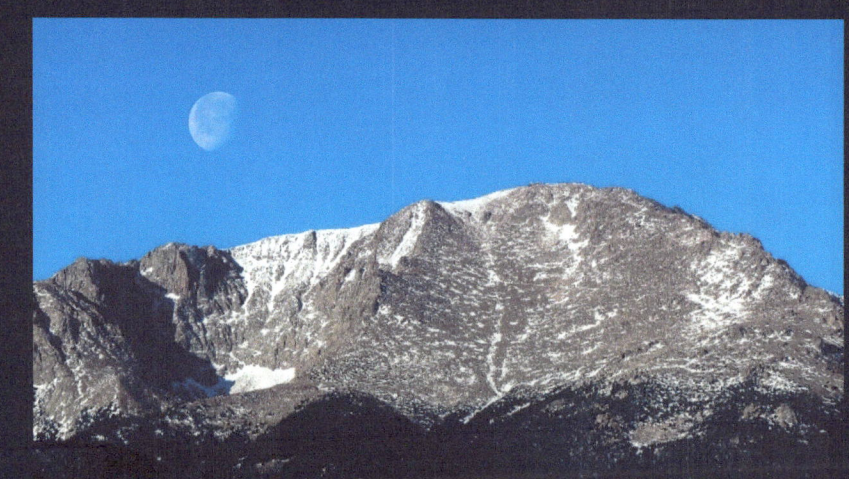

Setting moons
are just as nice
to catch
in mid-stride,
too.

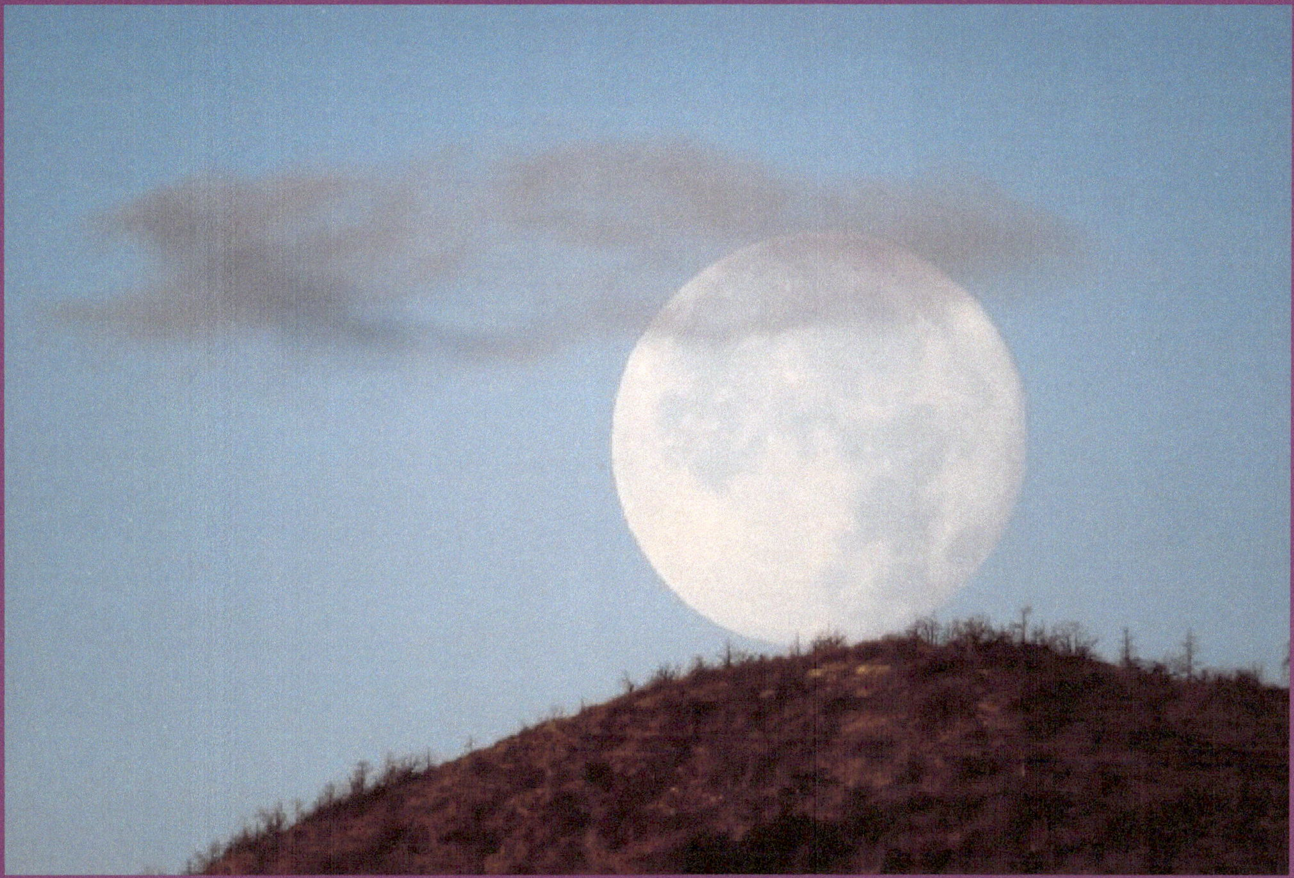

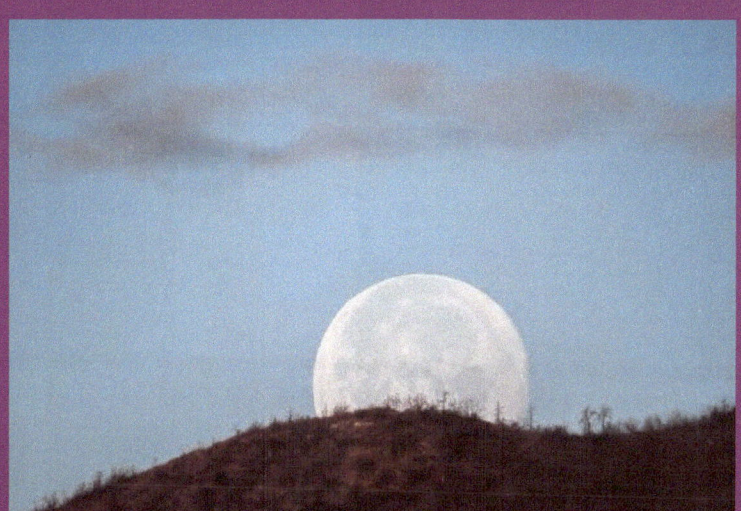

DECEMBER 4, 2017

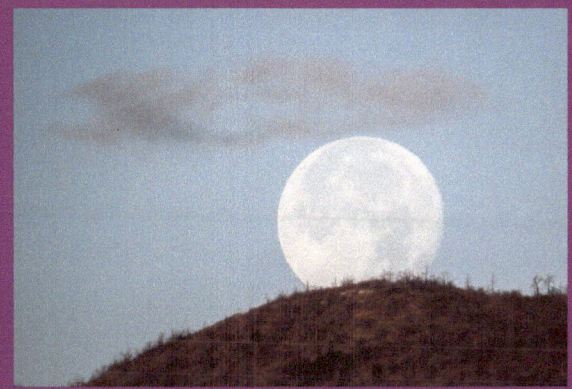

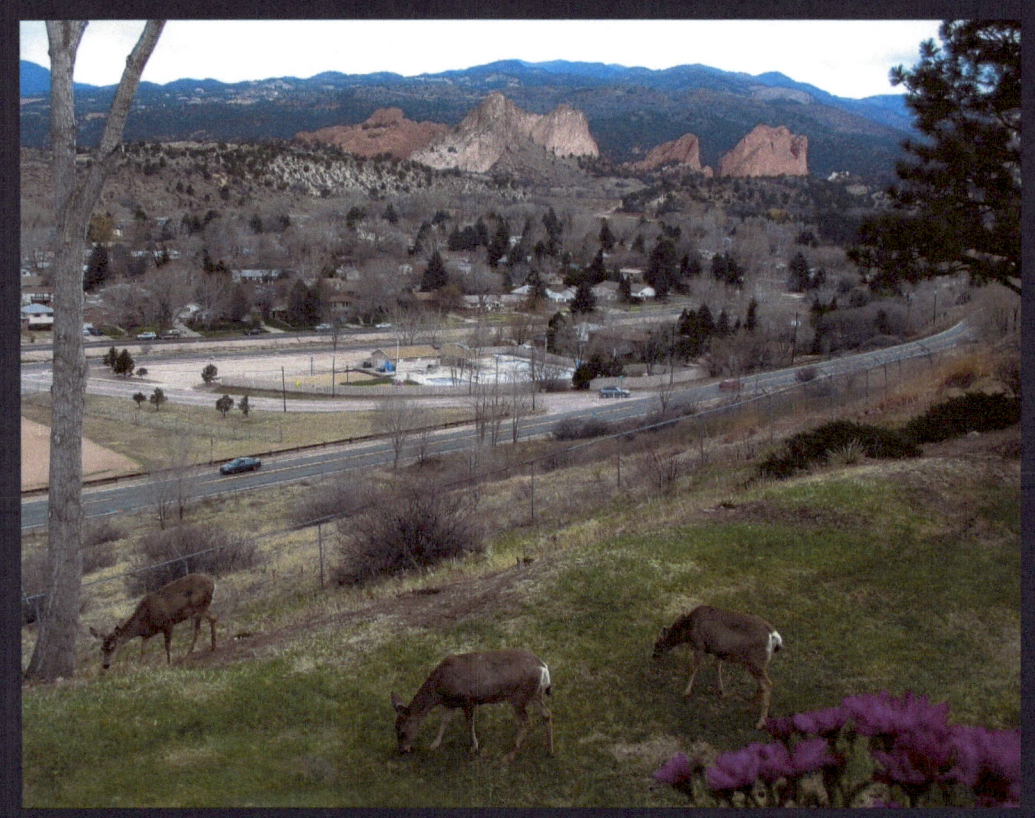

Often,
wildlife
come to
eat
at dawn
or after
dusk.

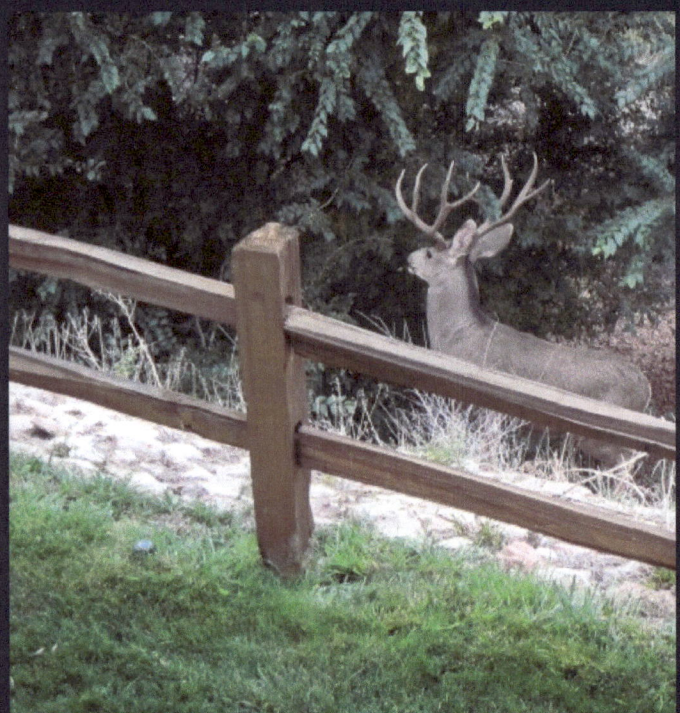

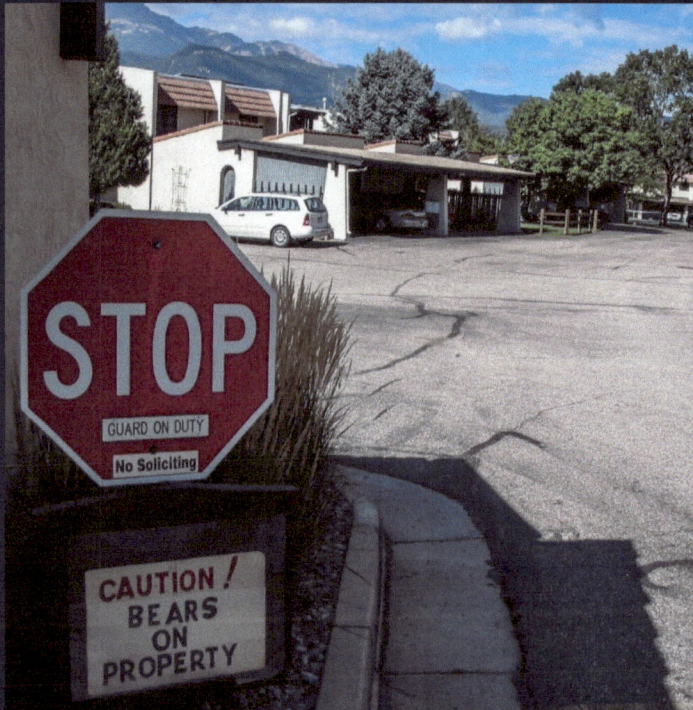

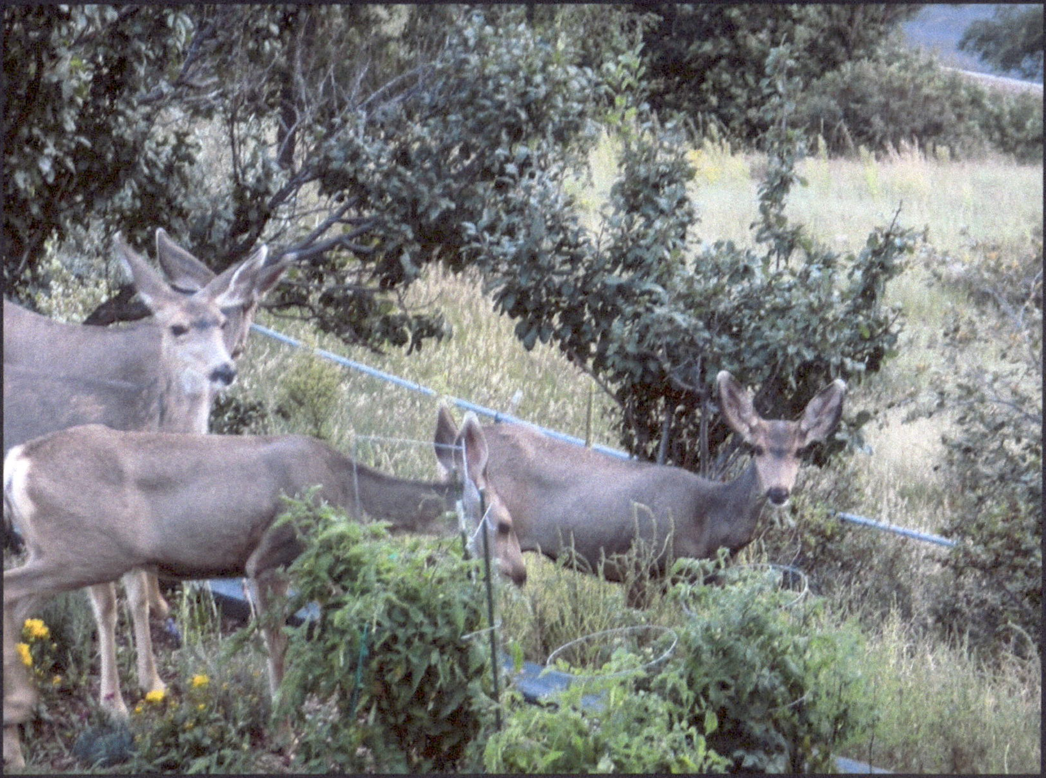
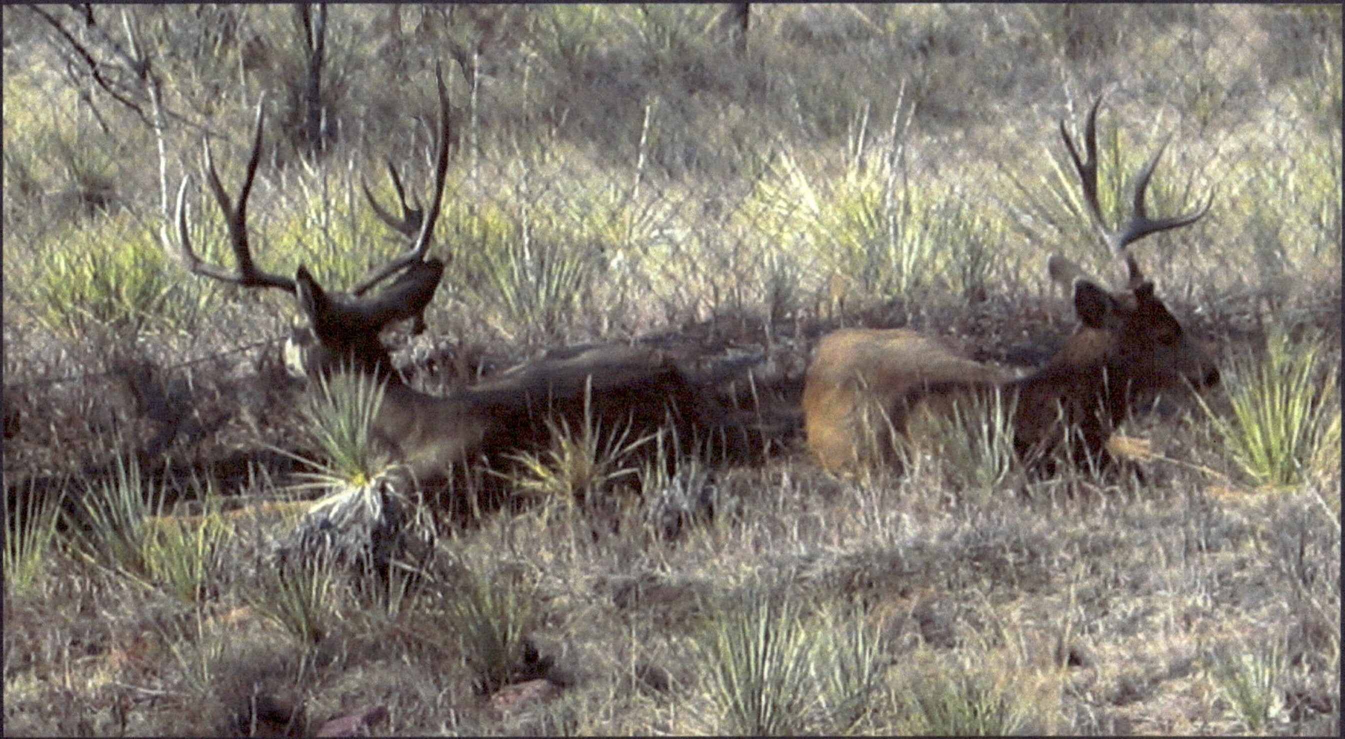

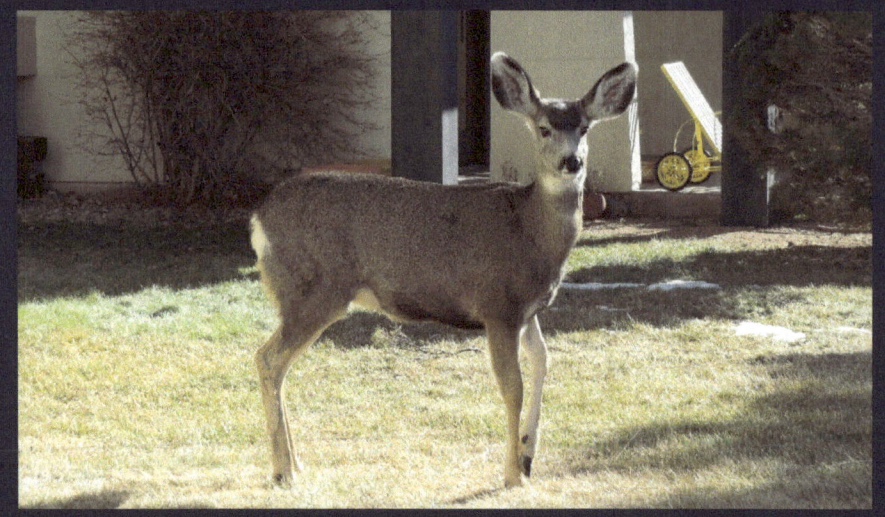

I hope these deer can catch the scent of bear and bobcat musk!

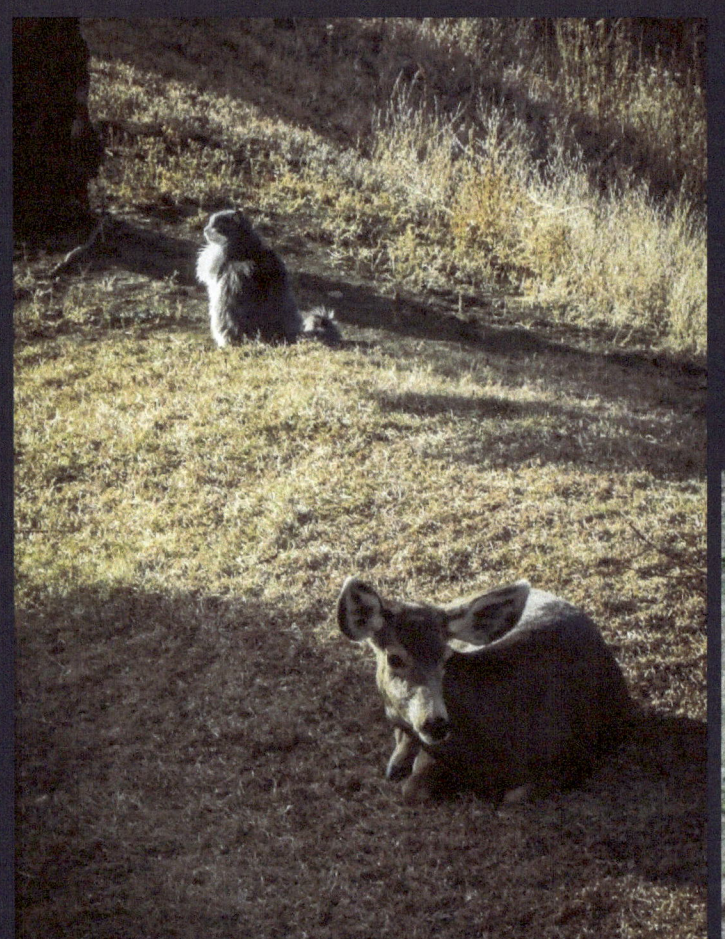

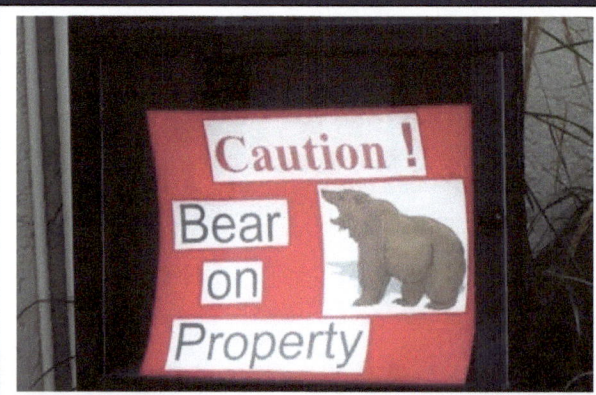

Caution !
Bear
on
Property

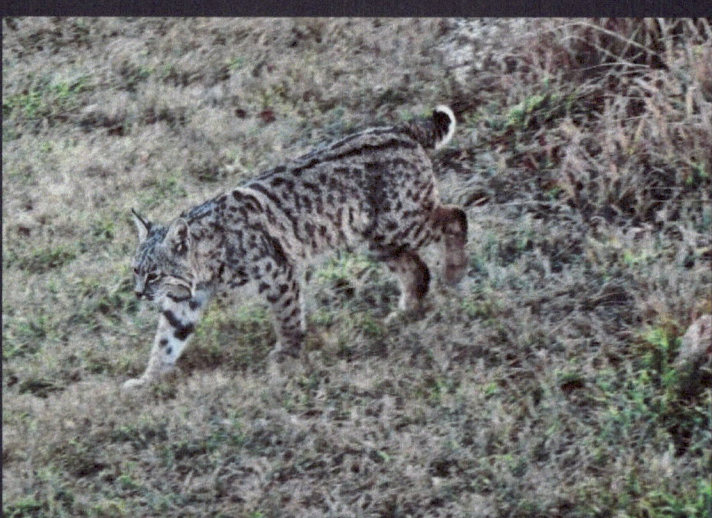

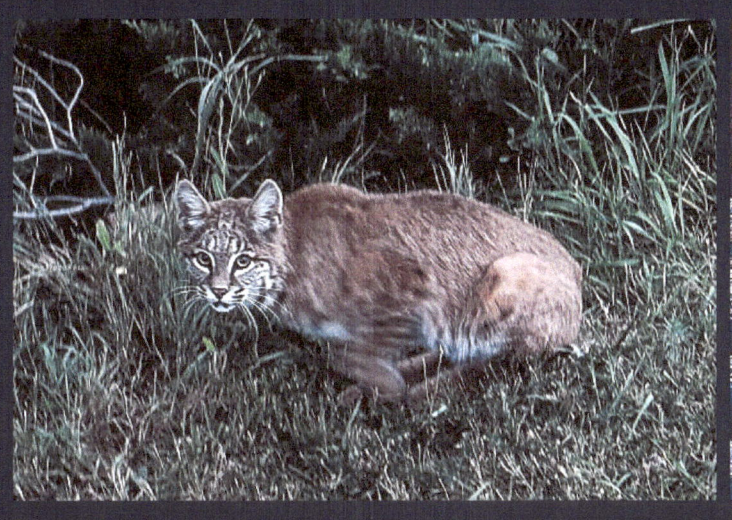
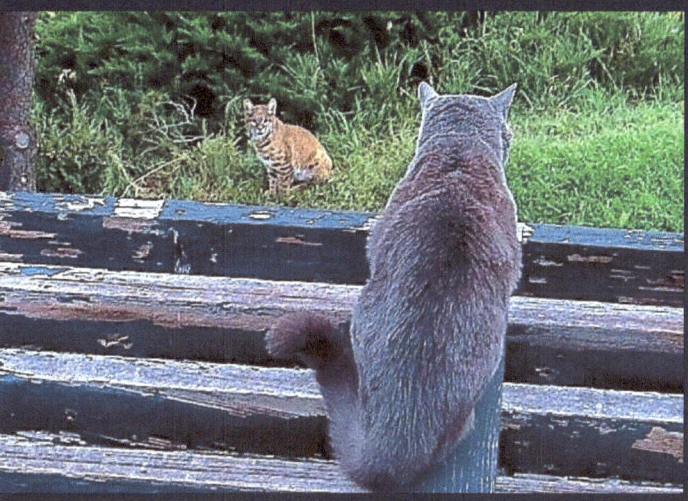

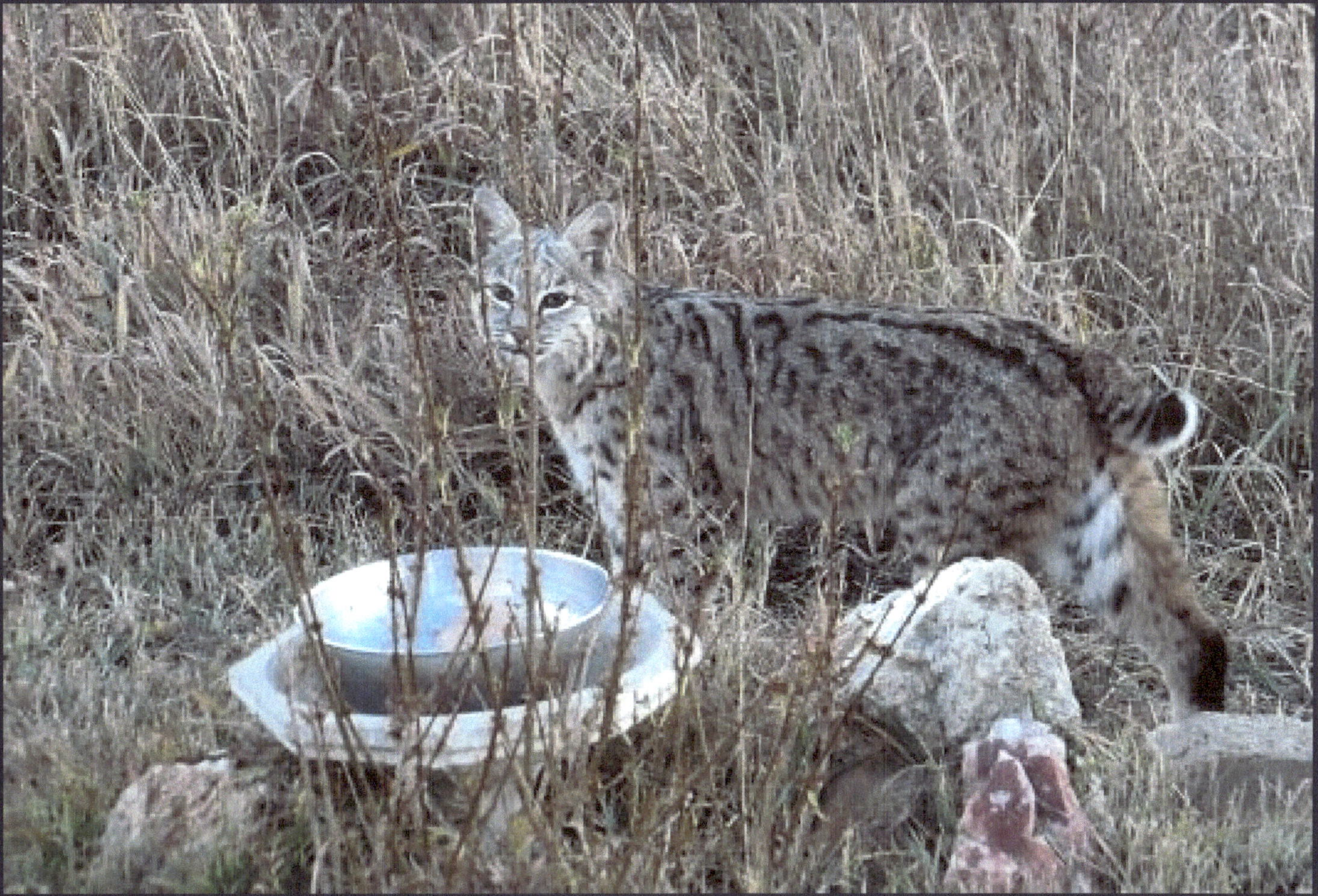

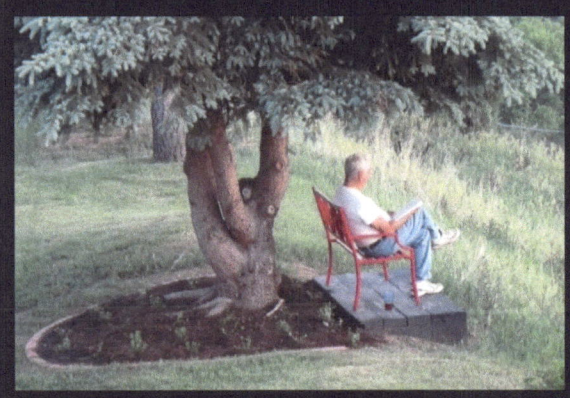
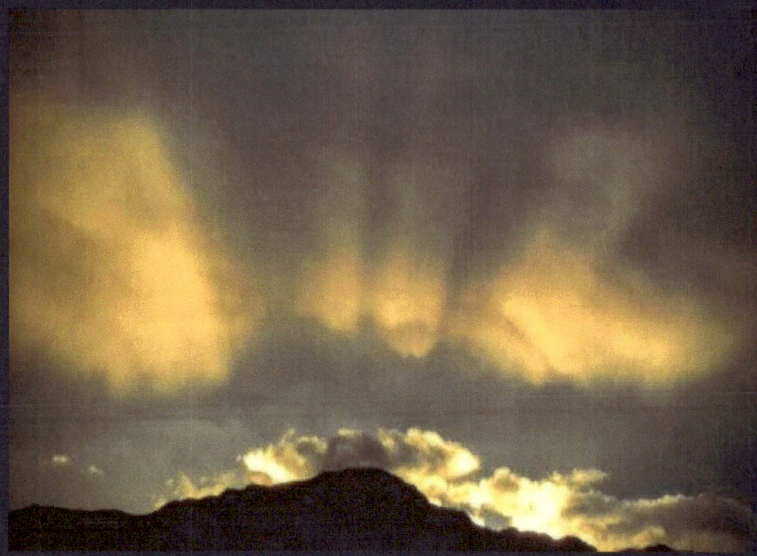
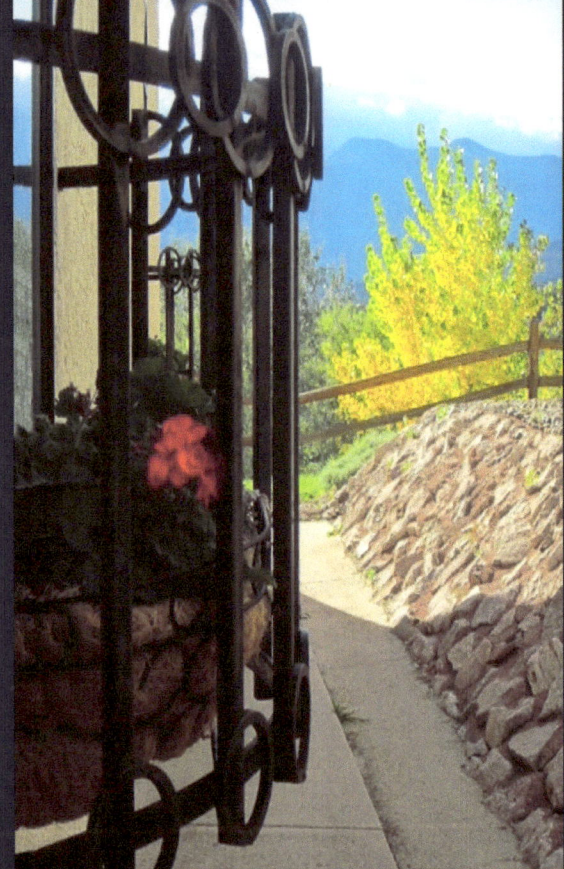
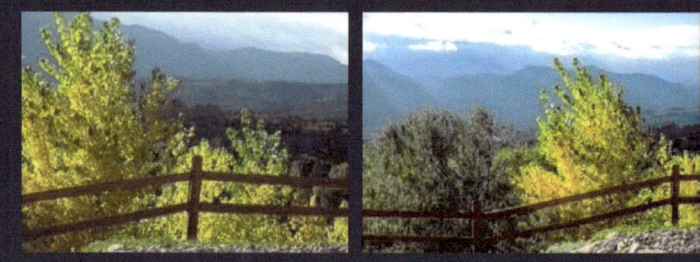
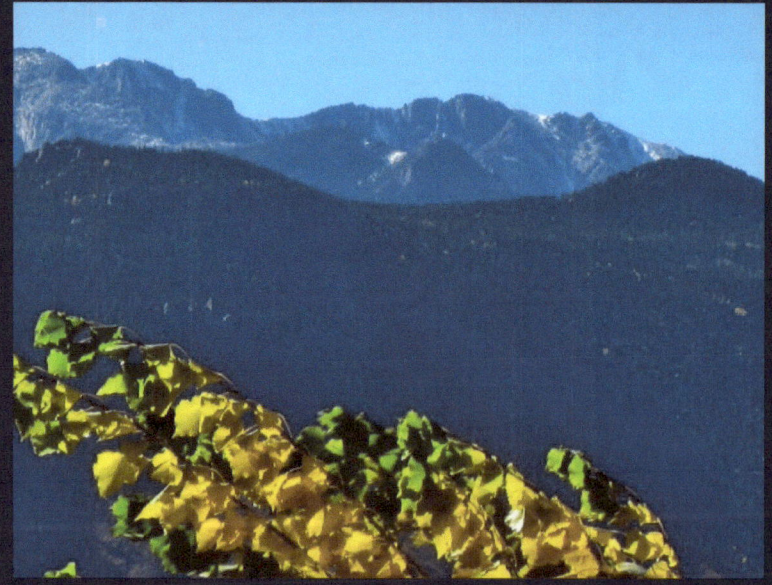

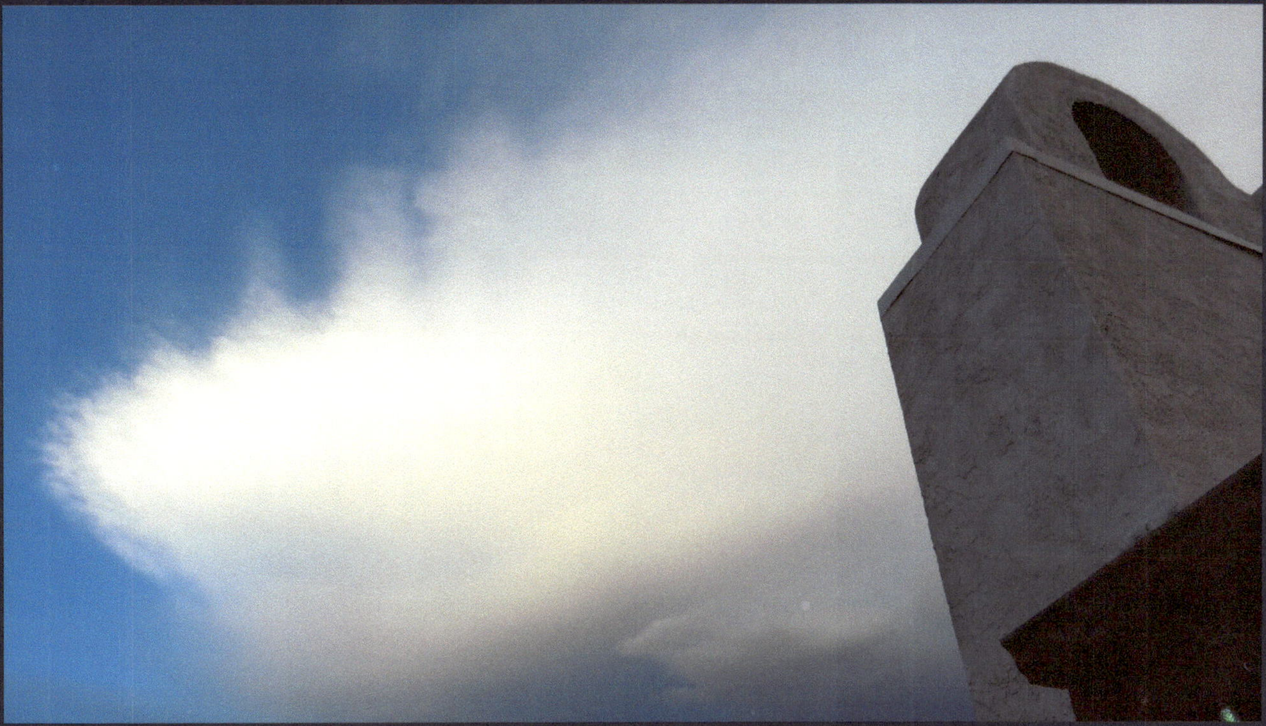

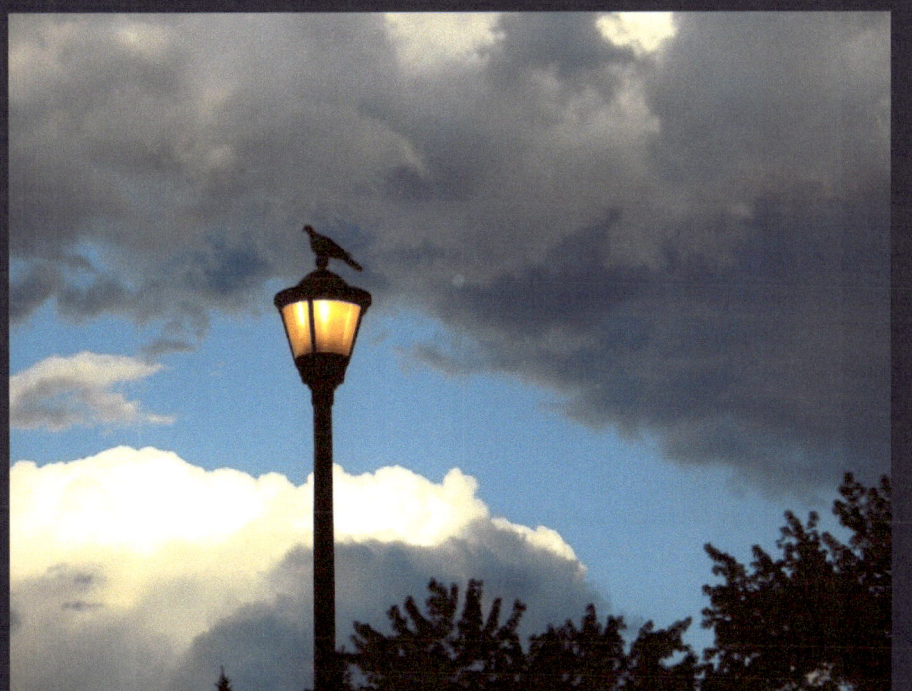

Watching a
sunset paint the
sky instills great
awe in me.

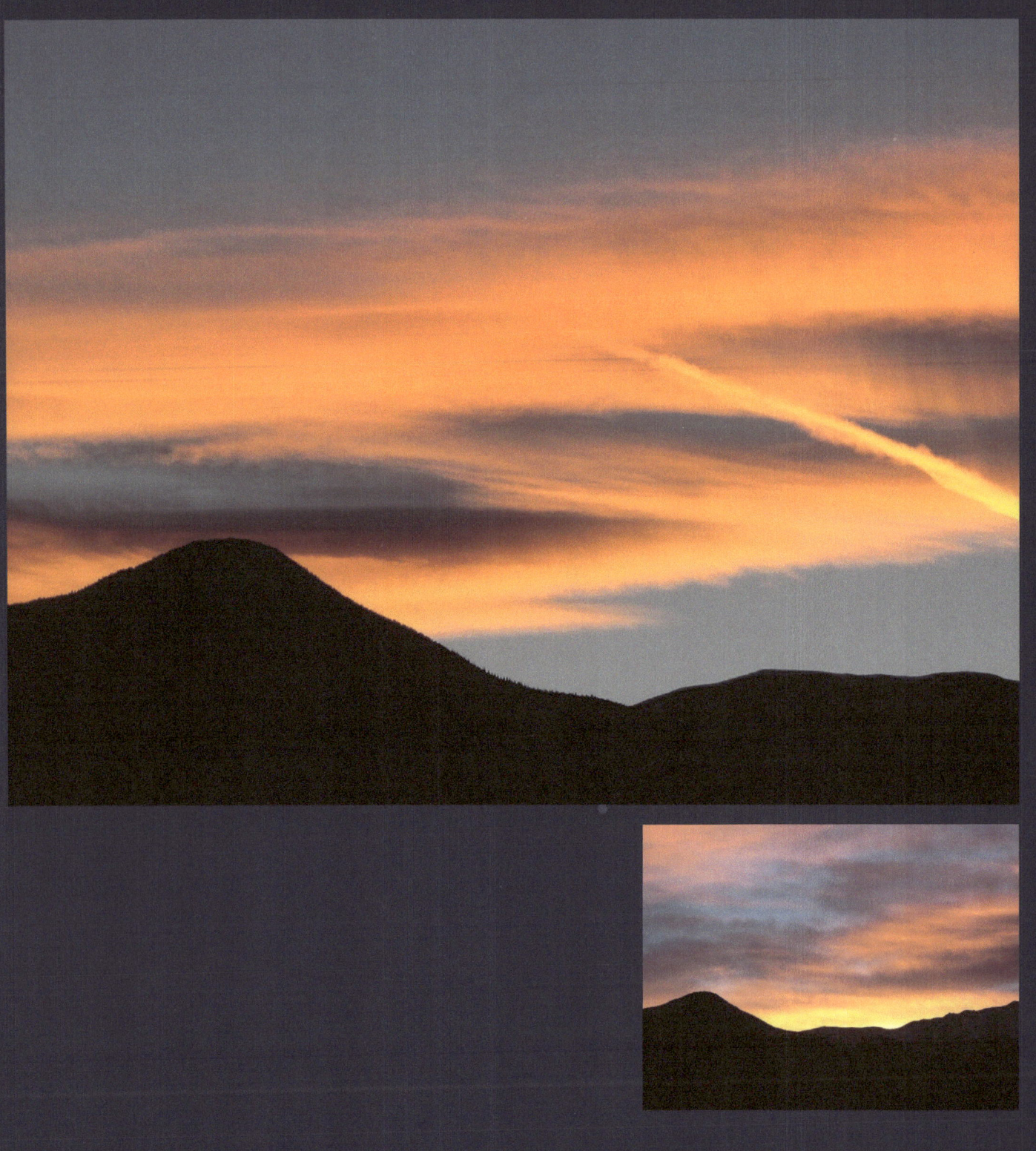

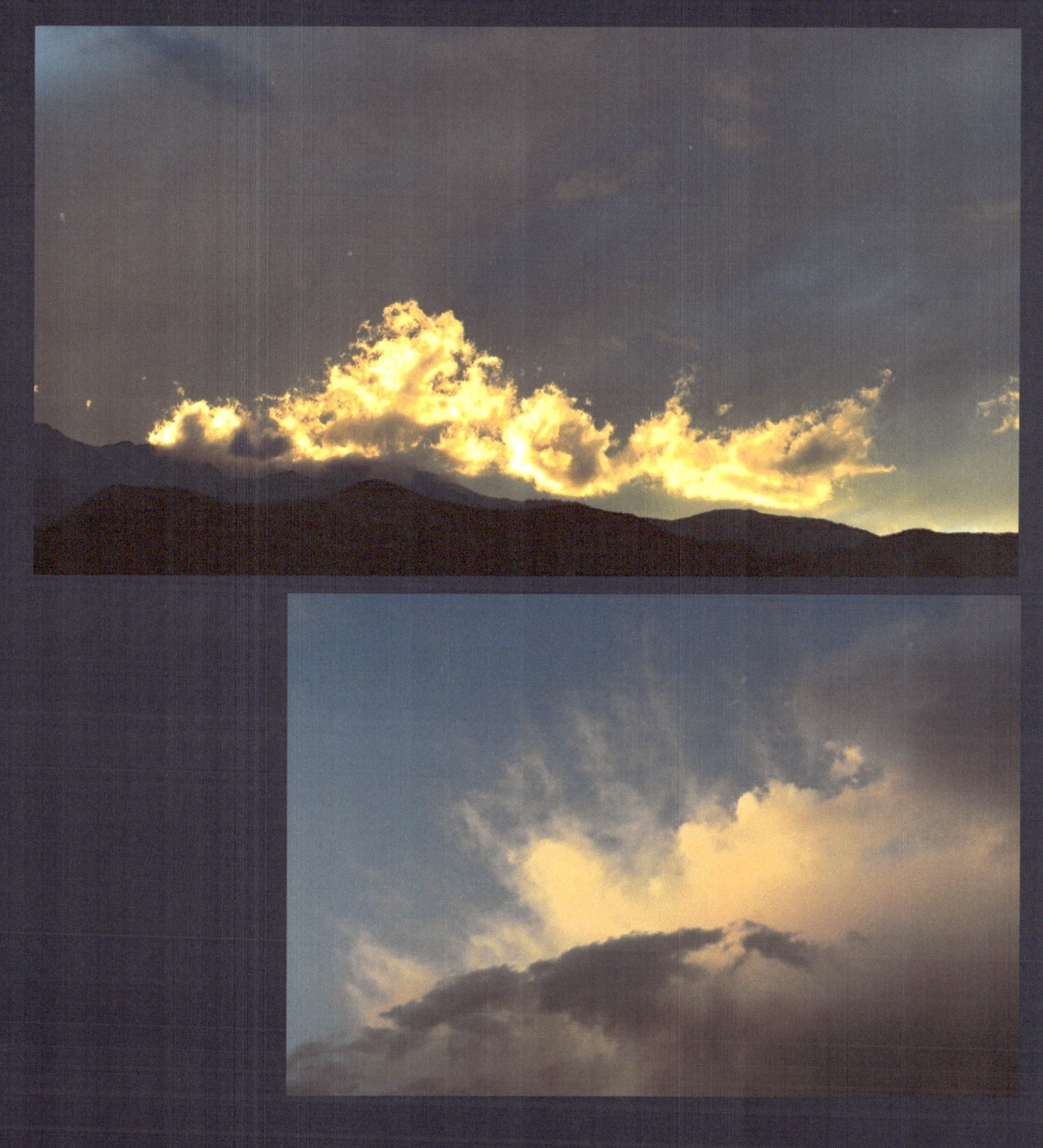

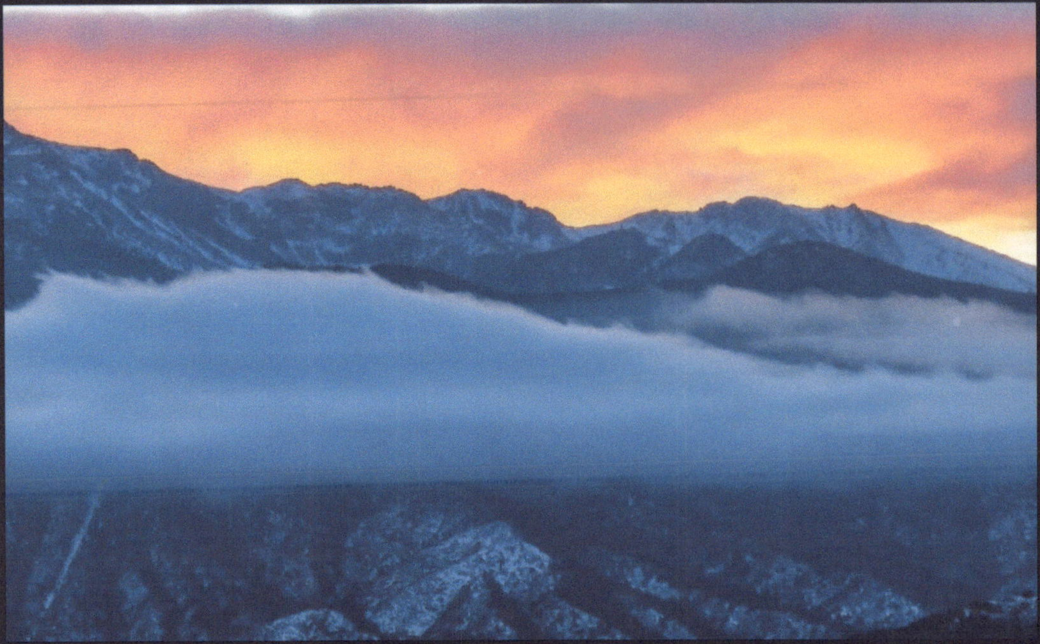

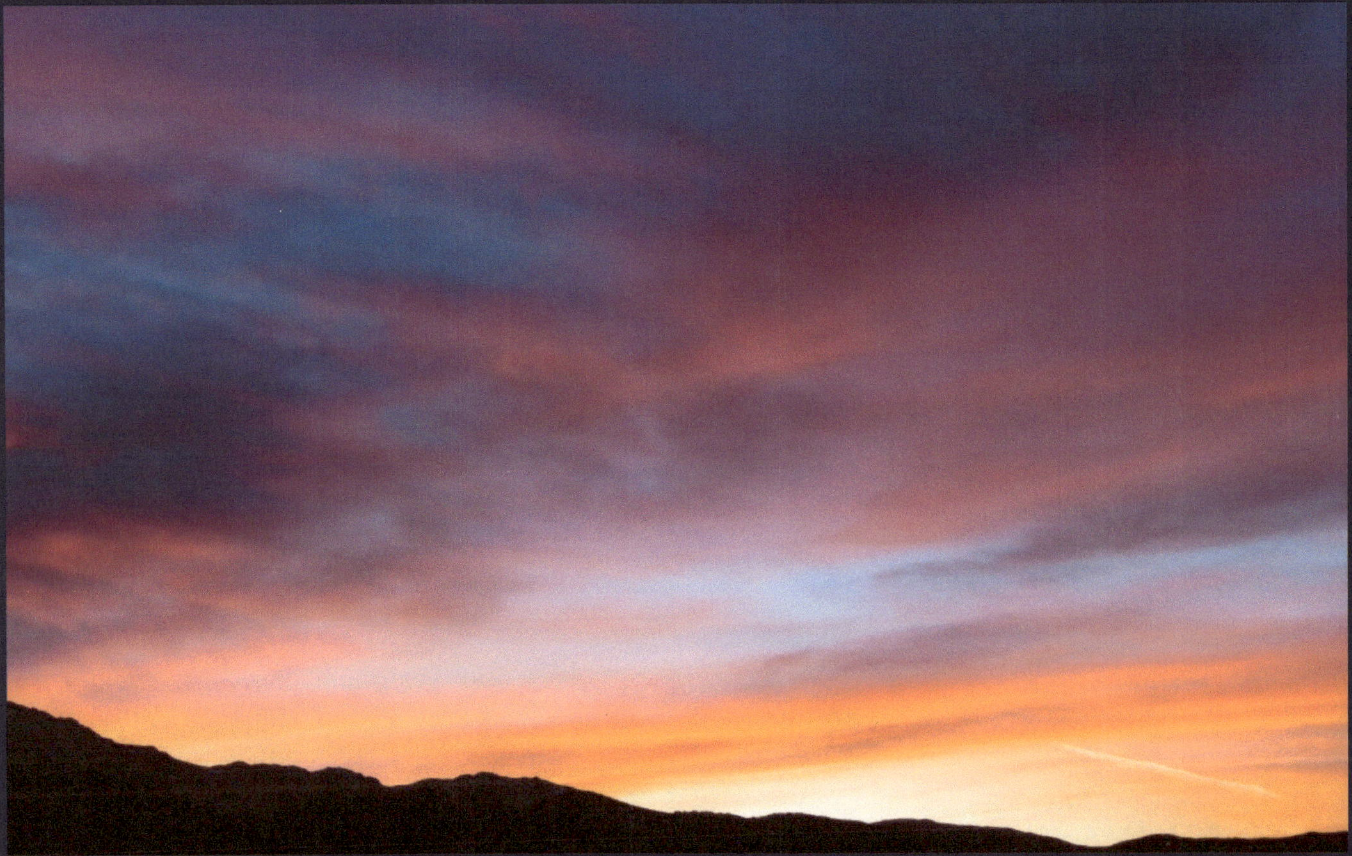

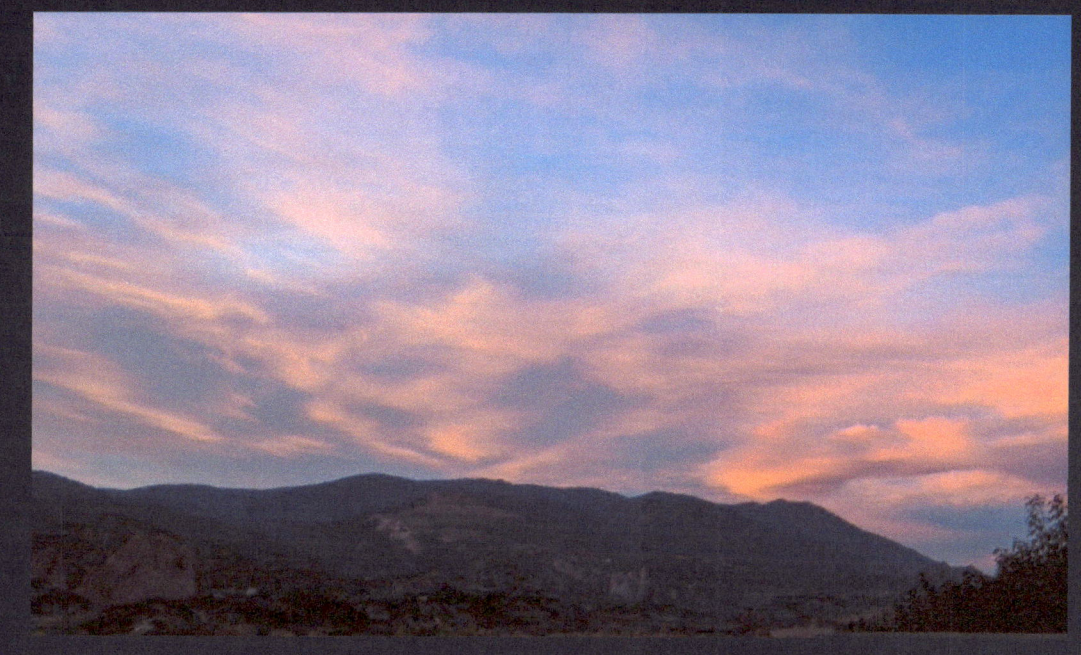

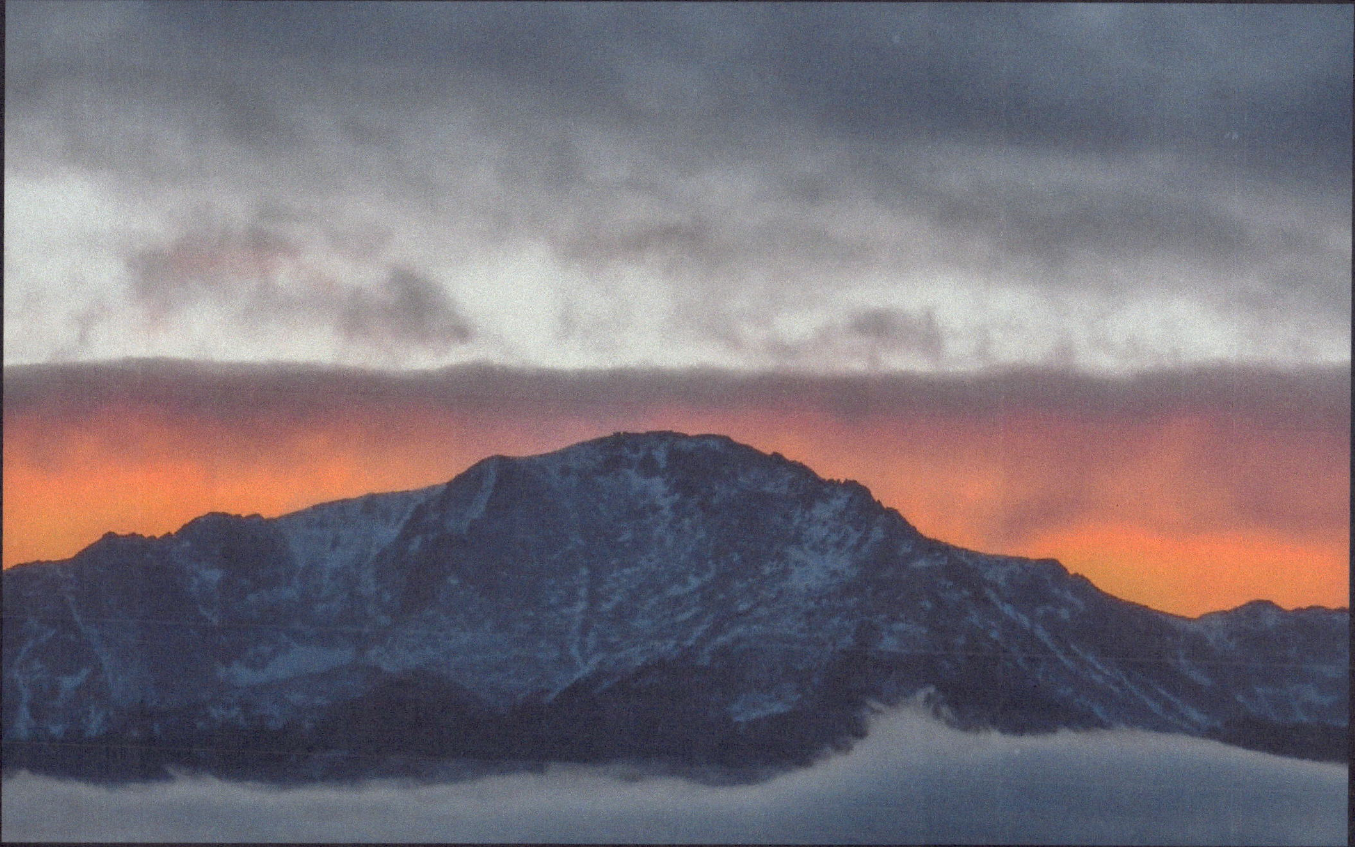

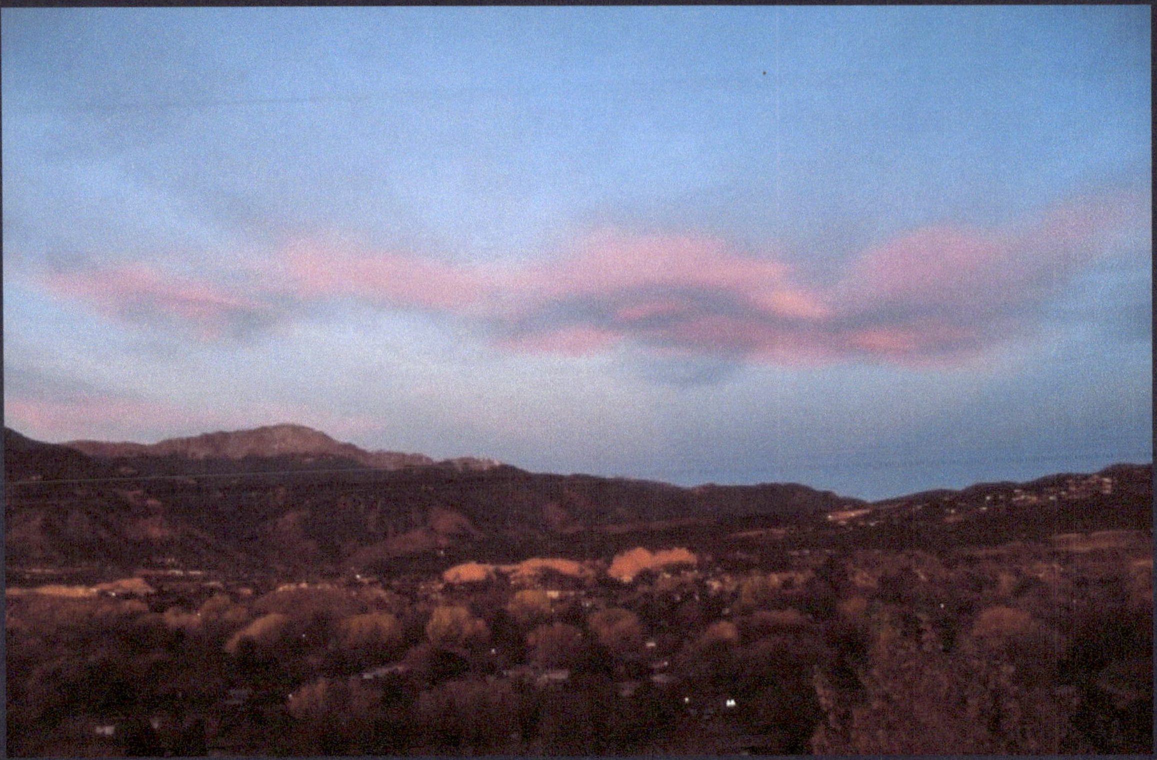

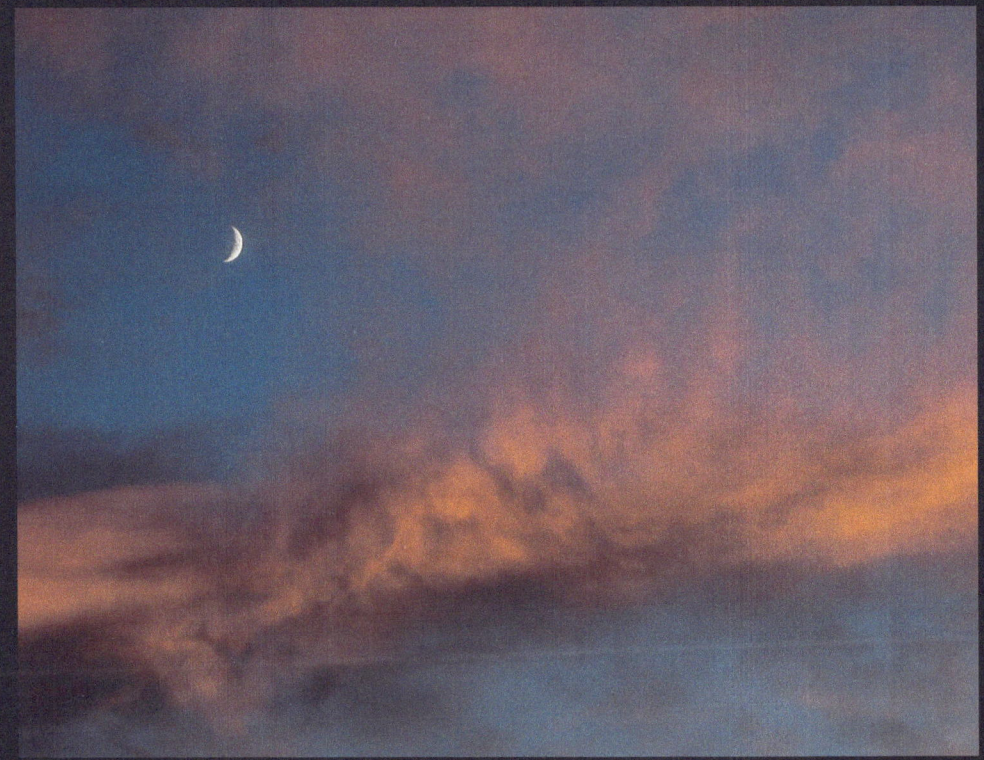

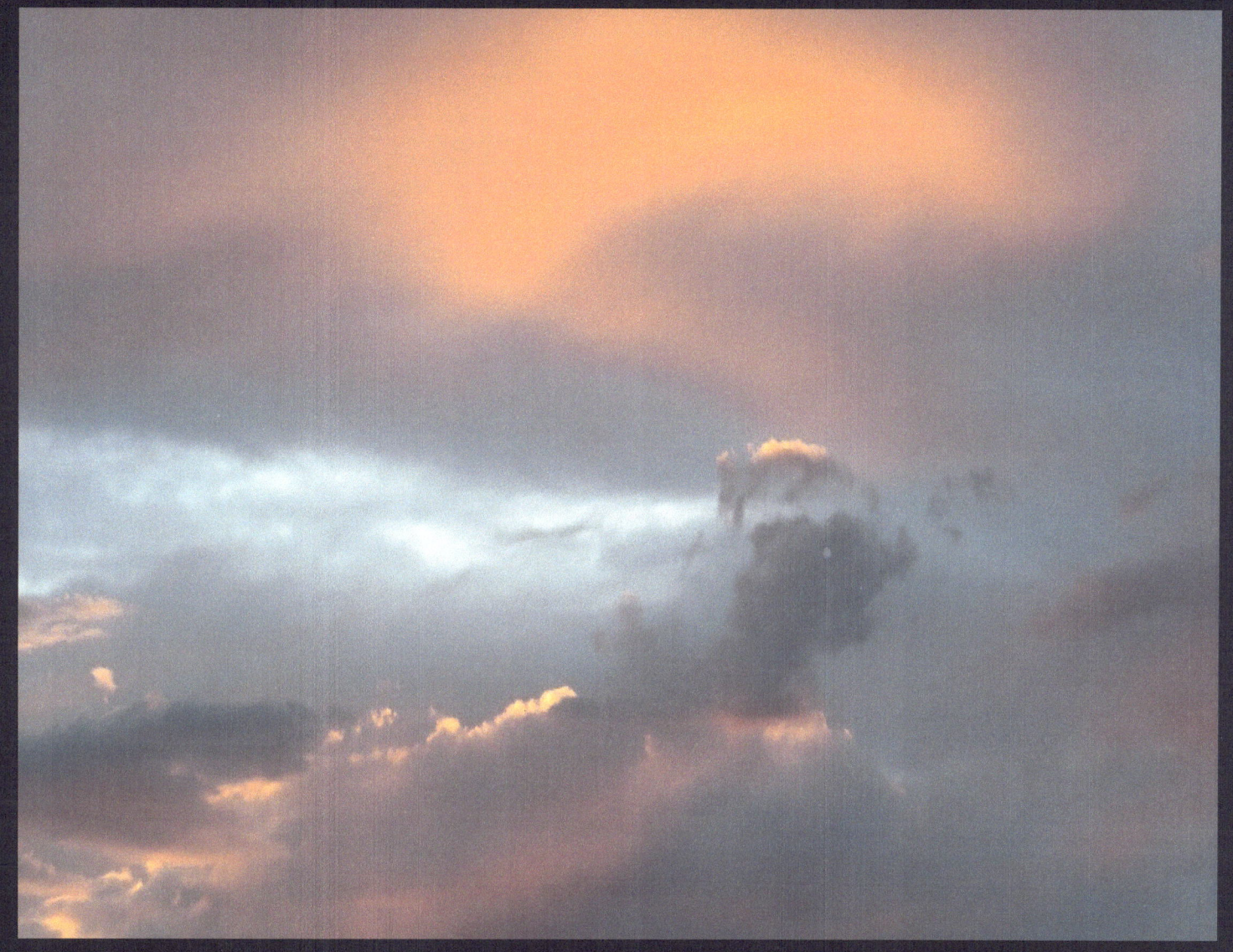

Can you say, with honesty, that you would not agree?

Echo Hill Arts Press

is pleased to make available

Impressions from Atwood

A Pictorial Diversion series

for Times of Waiting

https://www.atwoodcutting.com

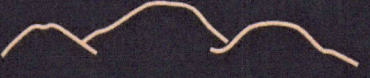

Echo Hill Arts Press

www.ingramcontent.com/pod-product-compliance
Lightning Source LLC
Chambersburg PA
CBHW050910180526
45159CB00007B/2859